# You Can Tell It's

## Humor For Those Who Love The Game

Inspired by Faith

You Can Tell It's Football Season
ISBN 978-0-9859685-9-5

Published by Product Concept Mfg., Inc.
2175 N. Academy Circle #200, Colorado Springs, CO 80909

©2013 Product Concept Mfg., Inc.  All rights reserved.

Written and Compiled by Patricia Mitchell
in association with Product Concept Mfg., Inc.

Sayings not having a credit listed are contributed by writers
for Product Concept Mfg., Inc. or in a rare case,
the author is unknown.

# You Can Tell It's

# FOOTBALL SEASON

## What's not to love about football?

A nip in the breeze, big-screen TVs, home-town pride, friends, family, and platters of food…and oh yes, the game!

This is a book of jokes, anecdotes, chuckles, cartoons, and trivia to tickle the funny bone of everyone from the passionate year-round fan to the casual big-game watcher. If it's football season, here's your source for some good, clean funnies to pass around, along with the Buffalo wings and chips. If it's not, here's something to read until it finally is time to get back to the gridiron!

# Ouch!

The football fan, on his way back from the concession stand, asked a fellow in an aisle seat whether he had stepped on his foot a few minutes ago. The fellow replied, "You sure did, dude," and waited for an apology. "Great," the fan said as he navigated past the man, "that means my seat is in the middle of this row."

# Suspicious

All during football season, Joe was frequently absent from his job. One day his foreman called him into his office and said, "Joe, I notice that every time there's a home game, you have to drive your aunt to a doctor's appointment. Can you explain this?"

"Gosh, boss, I never realized that," Joe replied thoughtfully. "Now you don't think she could be faking it, do you?"

# Big-Time Audience

Bill was known for his tall tales, so when he told his football-watching buddies that he'd spoken to thousands of people at the Super Bowl in years gone by, they chuckled. "So, Bill," said one, deciding to humor him, "what did you say to all those people?"

"Popcorn! Peanuts! Hot dogs! Ice-cold drinks! Nachos! Buy 'em here!"

When you are aspiring to the highest place, it is honorable to reach the second or even the third rank.

Cicero

# COACH'S Q&A

**Q:** What do you use to flatten a lumpy football field?

**A:** A gridiron!

**Q:** Why did the football refuse to play another game?

**A:** It was tired of being kicked around.

**Q:** What's the football game every cat loves to watch?

**A:** The Goldfish Bowl.

**Q:** What's the worst insect to have on your football team?

**A:** A fumble bee.

**Q:** When is a football stadium the coolest place in the world to be?

**A:** When it's full of fans.

**Q:** How is it that everyone understands when a referee places the football for the next down?

**A:** Because he lays it on the line.

# Oh Say, Did You Know?

The tradition of playing Francis Scott Key's "Star-Spangled Banner" at athletic events began in the early 20th century. The anthem opened baseball games as an expression of patriotism during the years of the First World War, and grew in popularity not only preceding baseball games, but football as well.

In the early 1940s, the opening anthem had become standard practice, however, the cost of a full marching band to perform it was often out of reach for smaller leagues. The accessibility of stadium public-address systems opened the way for soloists to deliver the anthem. Today, it just wouldn't be a game without the broad stripes and bright stars against a clear blue sky—and an entire stadium of people standing in thanksgiving for the gifts of freedom and country!

# Good Question

At the end of the season, the coach realized that his team didn't win any games at home, and they didn't win any games on the road. He spent all off-season puzzling where else he might take his team to play.

This suspense is terrible.
I hope it will last.

Oscar Wilde

I really miss our old tailgating days—
before Mark started dating
the party planner.

# What Happened?

The game lasted far into the evening, and a fan fell asleep in his easy chair in front of the TV. The following morning his wife shook him awake and said, "Honey, it's twenty to seven!" He woke with a start. "In whose favor?"

Games lubricate the body and the mind.

Benjamin Franklin

# High Fliers

The fans complained when their seats at the stadium were so high up that a flight attendant came by in the last quarter and advised them to throw away their cups, straighten their seats, and fasten their seat belts.

# Amen

The team hadn't won a game in ten years. One day, a minister took the coach aside and said, "Have you ever thought of leading your team in prayer before each game?"

"No way, Pastor," the coach replied. "We have so much to pray about that we'd be penalized for delaying kick-off."

# You know you're a big-time football fan when...

- You bring football-themed food to the office the moment summer training begins.

- You plan your family vacation around your team's playing schedule.

- Your season tickets are worth more than your car.

- Your newborn was brought home from the hospital wearing an infant-size jersey, helmet, and mouth guard.

- You paint your house in your team's colors.

- You buy your car depending on whether or not the dealer has it in your team's colors.

- You choose your wardrobe around your team's colors.

- You eat only foods that come in your...nah! Surely not...

# Coach's Counsel

At the club house, the coach walked up to one of his rookie players. "Roger," he said, "do you remember all the tips I've given you about blocking and tackling?"

"I sure do!" the rookie replied proudly.

"How about everything I've told you about good strategy, trick plays, and psyching out the opposing team?"

"Yep—every word of it!"

"Well, son," the coach said, "try to forget it. You've been traded."

# Rough Season

"I don't mind turning 50," the football coach told his wife. "It's just that at the beginning of the season, I was only 45."

# Limited Eye Sight

Our team's referee describes a typical football fan as someone who spends the entire game screaming that he's missed a call at the center of the interior line; then after the game, she can't find her car in the parking lot.

Losers quit when they're tired. Winners quit when they've won.

Author Unknown

# Do's and Don'ts of Football and Life

---

## DO

- Get on the field and play hard.

- Tackle problems that come your way.

- Have a strategy for meeting opposition.

- Rely on the strength and abilities of others.

- Block fear and doubt.

- Expect to win.

# DON'T

- Fumble your opportunities.

- Listen to criticism from Monday-morning quarterbacks.

- Stop trying when the score isn't in your favor.

- Let down your team.

- Attempt to go it alone.

- Forget the rules.

# Food Fun

The one thing bigger than my stomach is my appetite.

The football player went to the doctor with an obstruction in his throat. The doctor extracted an entire pizza.

The football player pulled his chair over to the buffet table, and the manager came over to him. "This is an all-you-can eat buffet," he said, "but I'm afraid you must eat at your own table."

The football player went to his investment advisor and asked, "What should I do about pork bellies?" "Exercise," the broker said.

The mother of two boys on the football team finds it hard to believe that any farmer could possibly grow a surplus of food.

Success is not final, failure is not fatal; it is the courage to continue that counts.

Winston Churchill

# He's Coming!

One Monday morning, the boss went to see one of his staff members. On the way, he noticed an entire row of uninhabited cubicles, and then heard the buzz of voices coming from the break room. When he got closer he saw that 10 of his best employees were analyzing the results of the weekend football game.

"Hey!" said the boss as he stepped into the break room. "Why aren't you guys at work?"

"Well, boss," volunteered one brave soul, "to tell the truth, we simply didn't hear you coming."

Ask me no questions,
and I'll tell you no fibs.
Oliver Goldsmith

"Hey, I'm reasonable.
I'll admit I'm right if you admit you're wrong."

## You know your team is not doing well when...

- The marching band spells out SOS at halftime.

- Instead of a highlight video, your team's website features a highlight snapshot.

- The coach opts for an assumed name.

- The opposing team starts celebrating before the end of the first quarter.

- Your team's logo T-shirts go on the half-price rack during the game.

- Your kids rush over to the opposing team's players for their autographs.

- Instead of praying for a win, or even a tie, you pray for a point.

- Your dog refuses to wear the sweater you knitted for him in the team's colors.

# Beginnings

American football teams developed in the late 1800s, primarily in secondary schools. By the early decades of the 20th century, professional leagues emerged and enjoyed growing popularity in industrial cities along the East Coast and in the Ohio Valley and Midwest. It wasn't until the 1950s that the sport drew fans from coast to coast, and today the Super Bowl match-up is a must-see TV experience the world over, with intense interest in the innovative ads and big-name halftime acts...and oh yes, the game.

# Back to School

To impress her football-loving boyfriend, the gal spent weeks going over the playbook. But when she got to the stadium, she was astonished to find that no one had marked those little X's and O's on the field for her.

# Rookies

The longtime football fan commented as he watched the team line up at training camp: "They're looking younger and younger every year. Why, I'm pretty sure I saw a couple of them signing their contract in crayon."

Build momentum by accumulating small successes.

# No Can Do

A man and a woman walking along the beach came upon a bottle washed up on shore. When the man picked up the bottle, it shook and out popped a genie. "Wow," exclaimed the awe-struck couple. "Does this mean we get three wishes?"

"Sorry," said the genie. "There've been some cutbacks in my business. I can grant you only one wish."

After some deliberation, the couple decided. "Sir genie," said the woman, "we wish for world peace."

"I'm afraid that's a tough one for a genie of my limited experience. Can't you ask for something else?"

The man stepped forward and said, "Well, how about our home team makes the Super Bowl this year?"

"Oh dear," sighed the genie. "Let's go back to your first idea."

# Shhh!

A pastor pleaded sick one Sunday morning and put the assistant pastor in charge of services. Then he disappeared into the parsonage, changed clothes, and, taking the back way, drove off to the big game taking place in the next city. When he arrived at the stadium, he pulled into the parking lot only to discover that, being the 500th ticket holder to arrive, he had won free parking.

At the ticket office, he learned that there had been a mix-up with his ticket. Instead of a third-tier seat, he ended up in a prime position right at the 50-yard line. Then, in striking up a conversation with a man in the next seat, he found himself invited to spend halftime as the man's guest in the executive lounge.

Looking down from heaven, St. Peter couldn't believe his eyes. "I don't understand," he said to God. "Why are You rewarding him with all this after what he's done?"

The Almighty smiled. "Think about it," He said. "Precisely who's he going to tell?"

## Uh-oh

Everyone was really sorry to hear that the quarterback left school. Turns out that he couldn't pass.

## Conflict of Interest

The coach, angry that the ref had repeatedly ruled against his players, stormed up to him during halftime. "Oh, simmer down," said the ref, "you're just mad because we're winning the game!"

# Full Meal

The football player took his date out to the fanciest restaurant in town. When he ordered the wine, the waiter asked, "What year, sir?"

"Right now," the player said, "because we'd like to have it with our meal."

# A Little Uncomfortable

The rookie fullback was eager to impress. His teammates noticed that he kept his nose to the grindstone, his ear to the ground, and his shoulder to the wheel. How he managed to sleep that way, they never could figure out!

# Just Asking

The young grad, an avid football fan, was applying for his first job. The interviewer went over his resumé, and then asked, "What are you expecting in terms of a salary?"

The grad, who decided he'd ask for what he wanted, said, "Sir, I'm looking for a starting salary in the lower six figures, and a guarantee that I'll get paid time off whenever there's a home game at the stadium."

"Interesting," replied the boss. "And how about free parking, a set of seats at the 50-yard line, and a pass to the clubroom?"

"Wow," cried the exuberant grad. "Are you kidding?"

"Absolutely," said the boss. "But remember, you started it!"

Make no little plans; they have no magic to stir men's blood. Make big plans, aim high in hope and work.

Daniel Hudson Burnham

# Rah, Rah, Rah!

Over 150 years ago, a couple of Princeton guys got together and decided they wanted to perk up the crowd at their football games. So, from the stands, the guys shouted cheers and chants, inviting every-one—fans and players alike—to join in, which they most enthusiastically did.

Princeton alumni Thomas Peebles took the tradition to the University of Minnesota, where this new-fangled idea called cheerleading was an instant hit and quickly spread to other colleges and universities. For the next several decades, cheerleaders cheered from the stands, and cheerleading was an all-male activity.

It wasn't until the early years of the 20th century that cheerleading squads were open to women, but they didn't dominate cheerleading until the 1940s, when many men went off to war. Since that time, cheerleading has evolved—particularly at the pro level—from yells, chants, and fight songs to spectacular shows, including sophisticated dances and complex gymnastics routines.

# Dashed Dreams

There was a young fellow named Ray
Who boasted he knew how to play—
And so this past fall
They gave him the ball,
But sadly, he ran the wrong way.

# All-Nighters

The student said to his seatmate as they settled into the football stadium, "My next-door neighbors were yelling and screaming all last night."

"Keep you awake?," his friend asked.

"Nah," the student said. "I was so excited about today's game that I spent the night playing our fight song on the trumpet."

Ambition may be all right, but it sure can get a fellow into a lot of hard work.

# The Pigskin

What are those guys doing out there tossing around that pointy prolate spheroid? Or football, to those of you familiar with the egg-shaped ball used in American and Canadian games.

Early footballs were formed by lacing an animal hide around a pig's bladder, which explains how the ball got its moniker of "pigskin" (better than "pigbladder," wouldn't you say?) Today, footballs are produced to exact specifications with no animal bladders involved—though leather remains the preferred "skin" of balls used in collegiate and professional games.

# Just Following Orders

The football player had an injury and the team physician advised him, "Every day for 30 days, take one of these pills and walk a mile. Call me at the end of the month."

At the end of the month, the player called the physician and said, "Okay, now I'm 30 miles from home and out of pills. What next?"

# Ouch!

After a rough-and-tumble game, a football player went into his neighborhood pharmacy. "Will you give me something for my head?" he asked.

"Why?" replied the pharmacist. "What would I do with it?"

Sport is a preserver of health.

Hippocrates

# Big Money

A football player hit it big as one of the team's star quarterbacks. The interviews, guest slots, and product sponsorships kept rolling in, and so did the money. When it came time to get his wife something for her birthday, he asked her what she'd like. Being a thrifty woman, she cautioned him about overspending and advised him to get her something marked down.

So he came home from the mall with an escalator.

For a hundred that can bear adversity, there is hardly one that can bear prosperity.

Thomas Carlyle

# Keeping a positive attitude means...

- You keep cheering on your team, even though they're losing 12-0.

- You really believe that it's not whether you win or lose, but how you play the game.

- You subscribe to the fact that there's no "i" in team.

- You keep wearing the team's logo, even if that means having to explain yourself to your friends.

- You let a smile be your umbrella...even if it means getting a mouthful of rain at the stadium upon occasion.

# Rapt Attention

A group of football fans were riveted to the big-screen TV in the den. During the game, they heard a huge crash outside, but ignored the sound as they continued to root for their team, yell at the ref, and throw out advice to the coaches.

After some time passed, there was a knock at the door. The homeowner reluctantly tore himself away from the screen, answered the door, and saw a police officer standing on the porch. Behind him, the homeowner saw that his 75-foot oak tree had fallen across his lawn and driveway, burying half a dozen cars parked there.

"Didn't you hear that thing come down?" the officer asked incredulously.

"Yeah, we heard something out there," the homeowner replied.

"When did it happen?" the officer asked.

The homeowner turned to his pals still grouped around the TV screen. "Hey, guys," he yelled. "When did we hear that boom?"

"Think it was about three minutes into the second quarter," one voice shouted back.

# So True

If you believe nothing's impossible,
just try dribbling a football.

The road to success is dotted with
many tempting parking places.

Growl all day and you'll feel dog tired
at night.

Anybody can give advice—the trouble
comes in finding someone interested
in using it.

## Show me...

- A football player who has both feet firmly planted on the ground, and I'll show you a guy who can't get his shoes on.

- A fan who keeps her head held high, and I'll show you the ticket holder who never sees what's happening on the gridiron.

- A normal football fan, and I'll show you someone who thinks everyone else is weird.

- The fan who's in the office on game day, and I'll show you the guy who didn't like the ticket prices at the stadium.

# Driving Directions

Traveling to a faraway game, a bus-load of football fans got lost in the desert and were stranded for three days. Then, to their astonishment, they heard the barking of huskies in the distance. Soon, a sled arrived on the scene with an Eskimo at the reins. "We're sure surprised to see you," the fans cried, "but so thankful! We've been lost for days!"

The Eskimo looked at them with a worried look on his face. "So you think *you're* lost?"

WIDE RECEIVER

# The Field

A network of vertical yard lines across a rectangular field forms the familiar football gridiron. The pattern is based on field markings used on English rugby and soccer fields, yet grew into a distinctly American innovation in the late 19th century. Though marked in slightly different dimensions, playing fields in the U.S. and Canada are similar, defining the number of yards to the nearest end zone.

Gridiron, or "the grid," refers to the field, the term has become another way to say Football!

# COACH'S Q&A

**Q:** What are they going to use on
the first football field on Mars?

**A:** Astroturf!

**Q:** How come Cinderella will never
learn to play football?

**A:** Because she keeps running away
from the ball!

**Q:** Why didn't the dog want to join
the football team?

**A:** Because he was a boxer!

# Advice for football fans...

- You can always find the slowest line at the concession stand by getting in it.

- An easy way to get your lawn aerated is to let the team use it for practice.

- Don't put on your team sweatshirt while eating a caramel apple.

- If you wear your team's helmet and face mask, remember not to blow bubbles with your chewing gum.

- Don't disagree with the fan next to you if he's bigger than you are.

# So There!

After a particularly stinging loss, the home team's coach bumped into a sullen fan on his way to the parking lot. "Excuse me, ma'am," he mumbled. "No offense."

"And no defense, either, so it seems!" she snapped.

# DIYer

A football player walked into a hardware store looking for a flat washer. The clerk handed him one and said, "That'll be 15 cents, please."

"That's ridiculous!" said the player.

"Why, I can drill a hole in a quarter and make my own!"

# Do As I Say

The team's owner was being inter-viewed for a story in the newspaper. "I share my philosophy with all my players. I tell them that playing hard and playing well mean more, much more, than money."

"Is that the philosophy that made you such a wealthy man?" the reporter asked.

"No," the owner replied. "I became rich when my philosophy persuaded players to sign on with me."

Be like a postage stamp. Stick to one thing until you get there.
Josh Billings

## Signs the coach might be hard to work with...

- His "let's have a talk" means you have a listen.

- He believes he's right 100% of the time—and beyond.

- He expects perfection, although he'll settle for more.

- Your response options are "Yes, coach," or "I'm off the team."

## And a sure tip-off...

- The suggestion box in the locker room has no slot.

# Sure Thing

A star football player and his wife decided to go on a luxurious South Seas cruise during off-season. In a remote region, they were shipwrecked and thrown on a small deserted island, the only survivors. For days, they scanned the skies, hoping for the appearance of a rescue plane. They stared out at the sea, praying for the appearance of another ship. As time dragged on, they began to think about their beautiful home back in the States.

"So you made the house payment before we left?" the wife asked.

"Oh gosh, no I forgot," the player said.

"How about the payment on your BMW and my Jaguar?"

"Sorry," he replied, "it completely slipped my mind."

"And the credit card we used to pay for the cruise?"

"No, but I sure meant to—I'm really sorry!"

"Well, there's one thing for sure," sighed his wife. "They'll find us."

# Bow-Wow

After the football player signed a multi-million dollar contract, he decided he'd fulfill a lifelong dream of owning a pedigree dog. After finding one he liked, he asked the breeder: "Now, this dog has a pedigree, right?"

"Sure does," the breeder replied. "Why if he could talk, he wouldn't speak to either one of us."

# Bow-Wow II

The football fan was told he couldn't take his beagle into the stadium. "You'll have to leave it in the barking lot," the ticket seller told him.

# Winning Strategy

At halftime, the team was losing badly, and their confident coach got them together in the locker room for a pep talk. "Listen guys," he said cheerily. "All you gotta do is get a couple touchdowns here, a couple there, and we're headed for the win!"

Our greatest glory is not in never failing, but in rising up every time we fail.

Ralph Waldo Emerson

## You know that ticket prices have gotten out of hand when...

- The ticket office offers a monthly payment plan.

- You tell your friends you have them, and they ask if you've won the lottery.

- The bank won't give you a loan to cover them, even with your house as collateral.

- You can afford them if you don't have to buy anything else for the rest of your life.

- Your insurance agent offers you a policy to cover them in case of loss or fire damage.

# Team All the Way

The coach insisted that players wear the team logo on their clothing at all times to build team spirit and promote hometown pride. One morning at the gas station he happened to see one of the players at the next pump, and the coach noticed he was wearing a plain T-shirt and jeans. "Hey, there," he called to the player. "Where's your logo?"

The startled young man answered, "Sorry sir—I guess I left it on my pajamas!"

# Keep Practicing

"Practice makes perfect," yelled the high school football coach to his team.

"Easy for him to say," a team member muttered to a teammate. "He's never heard my little sister practice the trombone for an hour."

Most people never run far enough on their first wind to find out they've got a second.

William James

# No Match

The former football star decided to write a best-seller about his gridiron experience. Words for the bestseller came quickly and easily, but trouble started at the lack of best-buyers.

# Easy to Please

The rookie player assured the coach he'd be on the practice field bright and early the next morning.

"Good," barked the coach. "Either one would be an improvement!"

# COACH'S Q&A

**Q:** What do football players do off-season?

**A:** Sit directly in front of you at the movies!

**Q:** Which football player should get the biggest helmet?

**A:** The one with the biggest head, of course!

**Q:** Where did the football players learn yoga?

**A:** On airplanes, while trying to extract themselves from coach seats.

# So True

Few things have a shorter life span than a clean football uniform.

Most budding football players won't be able to handle stardom…but then, most won't have to.

It's not how big you are—it's how big you play.

The greatest oak was once a little nut who held its ground.

# Danger!

The middle-aged fan with a bad knee proudly referred to it as a football injury. His wife knew better. He fractured his knee when trying to move his huge big-screen TV set to a better viewing angle.

# Hot Dogs, Anyone?

In the stands at the stadium, a fan noticed that the hot dog vendor's hands were bright yellow. Asked about it, the vendor replied, "Can't help it. People keep telling me to hold the mustard."

Great boasters, little doers.

Proverb

# Lemme In!

Super Bowl tickets were to go on sale at the box office at 9 a.m., and people started lining up the afternoon before. By early that morning, the line, headed by a burly-looking truck driver, stretched around the sidewalk and out into the parking lot.

Precisely at 8:58 a.m., a nattily dressed, slim, short man walked up to the front of the line and stepped right in front of the truck driver. Incensed, the big man took hold of the intruder and shoved him clear out to the curb, much to the approval of those who had stood in line throughout the night.

The small man got up, dusted himself off, straightened his clothes, and again stepped to the front of the line. Again the big fella sent him flying. Twice more the small man got up and headed to the front of the line, and twice more the big man pushed him to the ground.

Finally the small man got up, straightened his clothes, and pointed to the big man. "Look, mister," he declared, "you shove me around one more time, and I'm not unlocking the door of that ticket booth!"

## The home team is so bad this season that...

- The only way they can keep their losses down is to pray for rainouts.

- No one's interested in free season tickets.

- Management has to rent cheerleaders from another state.

- The cheerleaders prefer to stay home and text their cheers.

- The artificial turf died.

# Fan Hazard

Throughout the game, Joe hollered
at the coach, bellowed at the ref,
and roared when his team made a
touchdown. By the end of the game,
his voice cracked with hoarseness.
"What do you know," he whispered to
his seat mate, "I've lost my voice."
"Not to worry, buddy," the weary man
said, "You'll find it in my left ear."

In things pertaining to enthusiasm, no
man is sane who does not know how
to be insane on proper occasions.

Henry Ward Beecher

# Tackled

Out on the field, it was big animals vs. small animals. At halftime, the big animals were in the lead, 7-0. Then in the second half, a centipede made a ferocious tackle on an elephant, bringing him down with a Thud! Time out! In the huddle, the small animals said to the centipede, "Hey, where were you during the first half?" The centipede answered, "Oh, I was in the locker room getting my ankles taped."

# Tuned In

Football season is when fans tune in the sports channel and tune out everything else.

# Threat or Promise?

The booster club announced to the team that they were behind the players 100%—win or tie.

# Eyes Have It

Before summer training for the high school team, every would-be player had to pass a routine physical. During an eye exam, the optometrist asked one young hopeful, "Have your eyes ever been checked?"

"No, sir," the youngster replied, "they've always been blue."

# Pssst!

The team was surprised when Coach Smith arrived at practice unable to talk above a whisper. Earlier that day, he had shouted at his kids through a screen door and strained his voice.

# Longtime Fan

"You must have seen some great plays in your life," the football fan remarked to the old gent seated next to him at the stadium.

"Sure have," the man answered, "but nowadays the game is usually over by the time I find my glasses."

Old age is when you find yourself using one bend-over to pick up two things.

If quitters never win and
winners never quit, why do you always
say "quit while you're ahead"?

# Dating Woes

Sue and Jim, a football fan, had been dating for over a year, and Sue was ready to talk marriage. Though he professed profound love for his girl-friend, Jim demurred when it came to the "M" word. Sue asked, "Is it that you're afraid of a long-term relationship?"

"Certainly not," Jim protested. "That's what football season is all about, isn't it?"

# Too Bad

"We were the team to beat this year," growled the coach to the players, "and it looks like everyone did!"

# Did you hear the one about...

- The player who insisted on 50% off his chiropractor's bill because he was a halfback?

- The college fullback who's been in the undergraduate program for 12 years? He can run and tackle with the best of 'em, but he just can't pass.

- The guy who boasted that he was a triple-threat quarterback back in the day? Yep, he had threatened to quit three times!

# Water You Mean?

The star quarterback was struggling through Chemistry 101. When his instructor asked the class, "What is the formula for water?" he quickly raised his hand, because he was sure he could answer this one. Called on, the quarterback answered, "H-I-J-K-L-M-N-O!"

"Where in the world have you ever heard that?" the frustrated instructor yelled.

"Right here in this room, sir," the player replied. "You told me that water was H to O."

It is better to know nothing than to know what ain't so.
Josh Billings

# Could've Been Worse

After the game, the coach stormed into the locker room. "Twenty teams in the league," he shouted to the players, "and you guys finish dead last!"

"It could have been a lot worse, coach," one player said.

"How?" the coach demanded.

"There could have been more teams in the league."

# Touchdown, Anyone?

The day after the big game, two pals met for coffee. "Say," said one, "did you watch the game last night?"

"Watched some of it," his buddy replied.

"What was the score?"

"0 – 0."

"Huh. What was the score at halftime?"

"Couldn't tell ya," replied the guy. "Second half was all I watched."

# Sticker Shock

"Season Tickets at Popular Prices!" screamed the ad. But when the football fan got to the ticket window, she saw they started at $5,000 and went up from there. "How in the world can you call these popular prices?" gasped the fan.

The seller smiled and said, "They're very popular with us."

# Ahhh-choo!

Football season is that time of year when you have to explain why it is that raking leaves brings on a cold, but sitting outside on a frosty afternoon to watch the game doesn't.

# You Are Here

The football player returned to the hotel and said to the desk clerk, "Excuse me, I'm a little forgetful. Can you tell me which room I'm in?"

"Sure," replied the clerk. "You are in the lobby."

# Strong Muscles

The hard-driving coach's exercise regimen was legendary. Why, in the locker room, even the flies were doing push-ups!

# More to Learn

The football coach was trying to teach his team of rowdy middle-schoolers the rules of the game. He was especially insistent that the boys learn good sportsmanship on the field. He thought he had made some progress when, one afternoon, a fight broke out between two players and everyone else joined the melee. Furiously blowing on his whistle, he broke up the fight, scattering the team and separating the two culprits. "Now, which one of you started this fight?" he demanded.

"It's not my fault," one of the boys whined. "The fight started when he kicked me back!"

# Compatible (Not!)

The evening wasn't going well for Meg and Bob. When Bob brought up the subject of football, Meg snapped back with, "I think football is the stupidest game I've ever seen!"

In an effort to pacify his prickly date, Bob said, "Oh, I completely agree. I'm really glad there are 12 hours, 10 minutes, and 43 seconds before I have to watch another one."

# Tell the Truth

The minister reprimanded a young boy, having heard that he skipped church so he could get to the football stadium for the big game. "That's not true, Pastor," protested the boy, "and I have the fish to prove it!"

# Don't Do It

Cleaning the kitchen floor before your son comes home from football practice is like shoveling the sidewalk before it stops snowing.

# Phew!

The guys on the football team kept a ferret in the locker room. Though the smell was terrible, the ferret eventually got used to it.

Buying season tickets online is educational—you learn how to get rid of your money in a click.

# Just Bein' Nosy

The star player was being interviewed for an article in the campus gazette. "Ever break your nose?" asked the interviewer.

"Nah, never," the player replied. "But 10 other players did!"

# Game Plan

Rick, an avid supporter of his college team, took Lisa to his school's football tryouts. During the game, Rick pointed to one promising freshman on the field. "You know," he said, "I think he's going to be our best man next year."

Shocked, Lisa looked at him in disbelief. "I can't believe you said that," she cried. "This is only our first date!"

# Rules of the Game

The first football games were matches between Princeton and Rutgers in 1869, yet no hard-and-fast rules for the game existed. For a series of three games, it was decided that the first would be played by Rutgers' rules, and the second according to Princeton's rules. Because neither party could agree on a single set of rules, the third game never happened!

# Good Habit

A few minutes before every game, the quarterback cracked open his locker, peeked in, and then shut it. This went on season after season, puzzling his teammates. Finally they could stand it no longer, and one player sneaked up behind the quarterback just as he opened the locker door. There he glimpsed a single piece of paper:

**X = us**
**O = them**

# Diagnosis

A trooper pulled a car over for speeding. "Why were you going so fast?" he asked the driver.

"I'm sick, officer!"

The trooper, seeing the man's home team hat, face paint, and T-shirt and noticing a folding chair and cooler in the back seat, said, "It looks to me like you're a football fanatic and you're headed to the stadium for this afternoon's game."

"Yep, officer, that's a sickness of mine!"

Football isn't a matter of life and death—it's a lot more important than that.

# Rather Watch Football

"Yep, football's for me," said Tom to his buddy. "In fact, I'd rather watch football than eat."

"Really?" replied his buddy. "So what's your wife think of that?"

"She doesn't mind," said Tom, "because she'd rather watch football than cook!"

# Good Question

Why do people think Marconi was such a genius when he invented the radio? Why, there weren't even any football games to listen to!

Lord, grant that I may always desire more than I can accomplish.

Michelangelo

## Your football career might be in jeopardy if...

- Someone suggests putting advertising on the soles of your shoes as a way to raise money.

- They try to retire your jersey with you in it.

- Your most recent football injury happened when you strained your back while lacing up your shoes.

- You're running with the ball, and notice a snail is gaining on you.

- An aptitude test reveals that you're best suited for a position in the stands.

# Heaven Can Wait

One Sunday morning, the preacher gathered all the kids and talked to them about heaven. He described a place of perpetual peace, love, and happiness. At the end of his talk, he looked at the children and said, "Now who would like to go to heaven? Raise your hand!" All hands shot up except one. "Now, sonny, why don't you want to go to heaven?" the preacher asked the lone holdout.

"Because I've got football practice this afternoon," the boy replied.

Coach decided he might have
gone too far with cutting
his team's travel expenses.

# Did you hear the one about...

- The fullback who fell into an upholstery machine?
  *He's fully recovered now.*

- The coolest football players on the gridiron?
  *They were the ones sitting next to the fans.*

- The fan who always carried a football stats book in his jeans?
  *He was a real smarty pants.*

- All the fans who didn't bring an umbrella to the stadium, but not one of them got wet?
  *It didn't rain.*

- The fan who slept on a corduroy pillow?
  *It made headlines.*

# COACH'S Q&A

**Q:** What's a cheerleader's favorite color?
**A:** Yeller!

**Q:** If you've got a referee in football games, what do you have in bowls?
**A:** Corn flakes!

**Q:** What did the football say to the quarterback?
**A:** I get a kick out of you!

**Q:** What did the artificial turf say to the field?
**A:** Don't worry—I've got you covered.

# The Dating Scene

Lauren was delighted to date the school's star quarterback, but the girl, accustomed to frugality, was shocked at how much money he spent on her— huge bouquets of flowers, dinners at four-star restaurants, live concerts, etc. After this had gone on for six months, she asked her girlfriend, "How can I get him to stop spending so much money on me?"

"Marry him," came the answer.

# How Many?

The coach met an old school buddy one evening for dinner. After catching up on each other's family and a few mutual friends, the talk turned to work. "So," said the coach's buddy, "how many games have you won so far?"

"Well," said the coach, "if we win this weekend, and then win the next two weekends, that will be three."

The best place to put your troubles is in your pocket—the one with a hole in it.

# Just Don't Look in the Mirror

It's said that after many years of marriage, a husband and wife start looking like each other. The quarterback's young wife is worried.

# The band that played at halftime was so bad that...

- At least one fan thought the drums were carrying the tune.

- They started marching faster, hoping to move away from the music.

- Security responded to a disturbance on the gridiron.

- When the sound filled the stands, fans left to make more room for it.

Always imitate the behavior of the winners when you lose.

George Meredith

# Going Pro

Football was exclusively a college sport until August of 1895. That's when a Y.M.C.A.-sponsored team met in Latrobe, Pennsylvania, to play a team from a nearby town. The home team won 12-0, and players received a whopping $10 each.

In 1920, teams organized into the first pro football league called the American Professional Football Association, now the National Football League. Each of the eleven teams that joined paid a fee of $100.

# Football Camp

When their young son returned from two weeks at football camp, his parents noticed that he seemed taller and heavier. After he had showered, however, he returned to his normal height and weight.

# Gist of the Game

A father took his young son to the boy's first football game. After it was over, Dad asked his son how he liked it. "It was good," came the reply, "but I sure don't get why all the fans made so much fuss over a measly 25¢." Perplexed, his father asked what he meant.

"Well," said the boy, "everyone around us kept yelling 'get the quarter back, get the quarter back'!"

# How Cold Was It?

- It was so cold at the season's first game that even the clock had to rub its hands together.

- It was so cold in the stands that even the polar bears went home before the end of the game.

- It was so cold that vendors were selling ice scrapers to glasses-wearing fans.

- It was so cold that fans refused to go home at the end of the game—turns out they were frozen to their seats.

- There were more huddles in the stands than on the field.

# Perspective

The middle schooler longed to make the junior team, but he was failing history. When he complained to his dad about all the trouble he was having, his dad said, "I'm surprised. When I was your age, history was my best subject."

"But it was much easier for you," his son moaned. "Not much had happened yet when you were my age!"

# Avid Sportsman

"I used to watch golf on TV," said Charley to his neighbor one day. "Then my doctor told me that I need to get more exercise. So now I watch football."

# Need a Lift?

The man was worried when he stepped on the elevator, only to have half the football team pile in behind him. Fortunately, the elevator was going down.

# Big Guy

The home team's latest recruit is originally from Philadelphia—at least the first 175 pounds of him.

# Game Day

At the match-up between the hamburgers and the hot dogs, the hot dogs lost; it seems they were the wurst.

Exercise and diet are the best ways to fight hazardous waists.

# COACH'S Q&A

**Q:** Who was the fastest runner?
**A:** Adam, because he was first in
the human race.

**Q:** What goes up in the bleachers when
the rain comes down on game day?
**A:** Umbrellas!

**Q:** What do you lose when you stand up
in the stands to cheer?
**A:** Your lap!

**Q:** What did the dirt on the field say
when it started to rain on game day?
**A:** If this keeps up,
my name is mud!

# Did you hear about...

- The player who was asked what his favorite dish is? "Dinner plate," he replied.

- The eager young football player who couldn't wait for success? So he went ahead without it.

- The egotistical player who wondered how many great men there are in the world today? "One less than you think," his wife informed him.

- The fullback who was an inspiration to all young players? They figured that if he could make it, so could they!

- The fan who bet ten dollars on a football game and lost? Then he bet another ten dollars on the instant replay, and he lost again.

- The player who heard that an equal number of accidents happen in the shower as on the gridiron? So, to reduce his chances, he gave up the shower.

- The team that won a gold trophy? They were so proud that they all pitched in money to have it bronzed.

- The player who has a weird sense of humor? He sends teammates texts saying, "Ignore previous text."

# Wedded Bliss

The football player, wanting to impress his bride, said, "I just want you to know that I'm taking out the garbage." "That's okay with me, honey," she replied sweetly. "Please show it a good time."

Hubby was watching the game when he heard his wife say from the kitchen, "Sweetie pie, would you like chicken in gravy, savory stew, or creamed salmon for dinner?"

The man shouted back, "Chicken in gravy would be great!"

"Oh, we're having hot dogs, honey," his wife said. "I'm feeding the cat."

# One for the Record Books

The ambitious football player went to the doctor because he wasn't feeling well. After an examination, the doctor said, "Looks like you've got the flu, and a high temperature, too."

"How high?" asked the player.

"About one hundred two."

"Yeah?" replied the player. "So how high does it have to be before it's the world's record?"

# Who Won?

In Sunday school, the teacher asked, "Billy, can you tell me who in the Bible defeated the Philistines?"

"I dunno," said Billy. "They've never played against our team."

# Parental Orders

The older fellow was getting his yearly checkup and chatting with his physician about that weekend's football game. "So I understand you used to play," the doctor said.

"Used to," the old guy answered, "but I don't anymore. My parents won't let me."

"Your parents?" the doctor said incredulously.

"Yep. Mother Nature and Father Time."

# Great Guys

A teacher asked Billy to name the eleven greatest American men of all time. As the minutes ticked by, she said, "Are you almost finished, Billy?"

"Almost," said the boy. "I just can't decide on the fullback."


# Decisions, Decisions!

Two boys were walking home from school and talking about how they would spend the weekend. Unable to agree on a single idea, one boy suggested they flip a coin. "If it's heads, we go out to the stadium and see the game. If it's tails, we watch the game on TV. If it lands on its side, we go to the library and do our homework."

How about we compromise?
Heads, we receive—
Tails, you kick.

# Oh, Those Coaches!

Our coach does bird imitations—
he watches us like a hawk.

Our frustrated coach bellowed, "Now
what would you do if you were in my
shoes." From the back of the room
came a hesitant voice: "Polish them?"

Our coach has a fantastic ten-minute
motivational speech—unfortunately,
it takes him an hour to deliver it.

Of all the coaches we've had,
he's one of them.

## Invest Wisely

The hapless football player invested half his money in paper towels and the other half in revolving doors. He was wiped out before he could turn around.

## Like an Oak

The home team's beloved quarterback was like a big oak tree. He stood tall and wide, was a symbol of strength and stability, and sheltered anyone who came to him. Like all oak trees, however, he wasn't too bright.

# Lettered

The university team's coach gave him a letter this year, and that letter said he should try out for ping pong.

# Just Keep Breathing

The 99-year-old former football star was being interviewed for the sports section of the local newspaper. At the end of their chat, the interviewer packed up his notes and recorder, then turned and said, "It was a pleasure to be here, sir, and I hope next year I can come back and interview you on your 100th birthday."

"I don't see why you couldn't," the old man said. "You seem in perfectly good health to me."

## Just asking...

- Ever wonder what a football game would look like if all the players' knees bent the other way?

- How come sitting on a wooden pew for an hour is too much to ask, but sitting on a metal bleacher for two hours is fun?

- If four out of five football players suffer an injury during the season, does that mean one player enjoys it?

- Since there's yardage and footage on the gridiron, why don't we have inchage?

- Do you actually suppose that stretch jerseys have any other choice?

- Why is a player who signs a contract for $15 million called a free agent?

# Give Thanks

On the last day of summer football camp, a turkey strutted out onto the field. While the player watched in amazement, the turkey went up to the coach and asked for a tryout. The coach agreed, and then the turkey proceeded to catch pass after pass and run right through the defensive line. After a great showing, the turkey went back to the coach.

"So, how'd I do?" the bird asked.

The coach couldn't contain his enthusiasm. "You're great! If you sign up with us for the season, I'll make sure you get a huge bonus!"

"I don't care about a bonus," the turkey replied. "What I want to know is this: does the season go beyond Thanksgiving?"

Now have you considered the difficulties
that could arise in the years to come
from the fact that the two of you
root for different teams?

# Football Paradise

One day a football fan was visited by an angel. Seeing the heavenly being, the fan took the opportunity to ask a question that had been bothering him for a long time. "If you don't mind," the fan said to the angel, "could you tell me if there are football games in heaven?"

"Oh, yes," the angel replied. "There's a Bowl game every weekend, every seat is on the 50-yard line, you can visit the club house any time you want, and all the food and beverages are free!"

The fan's eyes lit up. "Wow!" he cried, "that's great news!"

"Uh huh. But there's something else," the angel added. "I see you have a ticket for the next game."

# Taxing Issue

The newly wealthy football player was aghast to see how much money he owed the IRS. Hoping to console him, his girlfriend said, "You should be proud to live in this great country that has given you so many opportunities, and pay your taxes with a smile."

"I would," moaned the player, "but they keep insisting on money."

Tax loopholes are like parking spaces—they all seem to disappear by the time you get there.

# Shredded

A player named Pete said his cleats
Would never come off of his feets—
When he climbed into bed,
His wife turned and said,
"I see why we've ribbons for sheets!"

# Some Things Don't Lie

The expensive hairpiece took ten years off the aging quarterback's appearance, but he found out that it didn't mean anything to a long flight of stairs.

# Path to Excellence

To be a successful football player, you need to work like a dog, eat like a horse, think like a fox, run like a rabbit...and visit your veterinarian once a year.

# Can't Deny It

Reading makes for a well-rounded person. So does sitting in front of the TV watching the Super Bowl with a tray full of snacks.

# The Father of Football

Walter Camp is considered the "Father of Football." Born in 1859 in New Britain, Connecticut, he later studied medicine and business at Yale, and played football. After graduation, he served as athletic director and head advisory football coach at Yale. Camp was instrumental in advancing football from its beginnings in rugby and soccer by defining the rules of American football. The game's official rules continued to evolve through the early years of the 20th century until becoming what we know as standard practice today.

# Way to Go

The coach, at his wit's end, yelled at a new recruit: "Smith, how can you make so many mistakes in one day?" Smith: "I get up early."

# Think Positive

Tommy was the strongest player on the football team, but his grades weren't where they needed to be. His coach, anxious to keep the boy on the roster, approached the principal, who shared the boy's most recent test scores. After scanning the dismal report, the coach said, "Well, with grades like these, he sure couldn't be cheating."

The most difficult part of getting to the top of the ladder is getting through the crowd at the bottom.

Arch Ward

# When It Freezes Over

A man approached the Pearly Gates and said to St. Peter, "You know, I'm so thankful to be here in heaven, but I've always been curious what the other place looks like."

"Oh, well, if you want to check it out, you're certainly welcome to do so," replied Peter. With that, the man was sent down a series of stairs that took him down below. Arriving there, the man saw a frozen wasteland with billows of snow blowing across big empty stretches of ground. Shivering, the man quickly turned around, climbed back up the stairs and arrived once again in front of the Pearly Gates.

"So, what do you think?" Peter asked.

"Interesting," the man replied, "but one thing really surprises me."

"What's that?"

"Well, I thought it was supposed to be filled with fire and brimstone, but all I saw was snow and ice."

"Oh," Peter said thoughtfully. "Must be that you-know-who finally won the Super Bowl."

The three great essentials to achieve anything worthwhile are, first, hard work; second, stick-to-itiveness; third, common sense.

Thomas Edison

# Another Option?

The longtime football fan went to the doctor, and after a barrage of tests, the doctor gave him a warning about his health. "It's not good," his physician said, "and the best thing I can advise you to do is keep calm, and avoid situations like football games that get you so riled up. Give up hot dogs, pizza, pretzels, sodas, and all that stuff you eat when you're watching a game."

The patient thought for a moment and then said. "Doc, now if that's the best thing I could do, how about the next best thing?"

# Hazards of the Job

The referee went to see a doctor about his ulcer. "You've got to stay calm," the doctor told him. "Don't get excited, don't let criticism get to you, and don't think about football when you're off the field." The doc paused, and then added: "So what about that stupid, ridiculous, completely unfair and obviously biased call you made at the stadium last night?"

# Sigh

The only heavy industry in our neck of the woods is our football team.

The trouble with referees is that they don't care who wins.

Our team lost six in a row, and then went into a slump.

Our team lost six in a row, and then went on a one-game winning streak.

# The team knew that management had chartered the wrong plane when...

- They noticed that the luggage rack was attached to the wall with duct tape.

- The guy who drove the taxi they took to the airport turned out to be their pilot.

- The flight attendant advised them to keep their hands and arms inside the aircraft while it was in flight.

- The guy on the ground used a dime to check tire wear.

- The Lord's Prayer was printed on the tray table.

It will soon take only three hours to get around the world—one hour for the flying and two hours to get through security.

# Good Time Had By All

The trooper pulls over a guy driving with a penguin in the passenger seat. "Say," he says to the driver, "is that a real penguin you've got there?"

"Yes, it is, officer," replies the man.

"Well, I suggest you take him to the zoo." The man agrees to do so, and he drives away in the direction of the zoo.

The next day, the trooper sees the same man again, still with the penguin sitting in the front seat. He pulls him over. "Buddy, I thought I told you to take that penguin to the zoo!"

"I did," says the man, "and we had such a good time that we're going to the Bowl game today!"

# COACH'S Q&A

**Q:** How do you make a hot dog stand at the stadium?
**A:** Take its chair.

**Q:** Why did the coach refuse to allow the kangaroo on the team?
**A:** Because he kept running out of bounds.

**Q:** What's the difference between a football player and a dog?
**A:** A football player puts on the whole uniform; the dog just pants.

# We Need To Talk

The boss called Jones into the office the day after the home game. "Jones," he said, "You requested yesterday afternoon off to go see your dentist."

"Yes, sir, that's right."

"Well then, how come I saw you coming out of the stadium with a friend?"

"Oh him," Jones said. "He's my dentist."

# Eye on the Ball

The rookie player came home with a huge black eye. "What happened?" asked his wife.

"Well, I was staring at the football as it came to me and wondering why it was getting bigger and bigger and bigger...and then it hit me."

# Double the Fun

The TV repairman came to fix the fan's television. "So what seems to be the problem?" he asked.

"It keeps showing double images," the fan said, "and I sure hope your men can fix it."

# Problem

A player from Scotland, McPhass,
Could run like a bullet, tackle and pass—
But the coach didn't deem
McPhass right for the team—
It so happened McPhass was a lass.


**All sports for all people.**
Pierre de Coubertin

# Years to Go

The team's doctor talked to the rookies about diet, health, and safety. At the end of the talk, he advised them to take a hot bath before retiring.

"That's stupid," whispered one player to another, "we've got years to go before we've got to retire."


# MVP

The quarterback was so rich that when he gets on a plane, his wallet is tagged as carry-on luggage.

# Honest Answers

The coach asked the young hopeful:
"So what do you run a mile in?"
"Usually shorts and a T-shirt, sir,"
he replied.

One teammate said to the other, "Dude,
you smell good. What do you have on?"
Dude answered: "Clean socks."

Boy goes to a security guard at the stadium
and says, "I've lost my dad."
"What's he like?" asks the guard.
"The home team."

# On Hold

Instead of a paycheck, the rookie player found this note taped to his locker:

*Your contract becomes effective as soon as you do.*

# Mind the Sign

This visiting team checked into the motel and then went to the dining room for dinner. One of them noticed a sign on the door:

*Shoes are required to eat in the restaurant. Socks may eat where they please.*

# It Happens

Two Martians landed on Earth and decided to explore separately. After a day's work, they got back together and shared what they had seen. One said to the other, "I came to this big place with a green, rectangular area in the middle that was marked out in yard increments. Around it on tiered benches were 75,000 people of all ages huddled under capes and blankets."

"Strange!" said the Martian. "So then what happens?"

"It begins to rain."

Rain is caused by big, high-pressure systems of cold fronts, warm air, and opening day at the stadium.

# It's Okay

Hearing that her son was back from football practice, Mom said from another room, "Johnny, be careful on the kitchen floor. I just waxed it."

"It's okay, Mom," came the reply, "I still have my cleats on."

# Footsies

His first time in the locker room with the team, the new kid was determined not to let on how nervous he felt. While putting on his shoes, one of the big guys pointed to him and guffawed, "Hey, dude, you got your shoes on the wrong feet!"

Incensed, the newbie replied, "No I haven't—I know these are my feet!"

**As the receiver said to the overthrown pass...**

*Soooo* long.